Wandering Woman: Iowa
The Ultimate Road Trip: One Woman's
Journey Across the United States by RV

Julie Bettendorf

Contents

Introduction

"Not all who wander are lost." *JRR Tolkien*

Are you sure? I thought to myself, as I tried not to panic. I was a long way from anything familiar, but that was how it should be. I had driven thousands of miles on dusty, pothole-filled roads. It's often on the worst roads that you can discover something truly amazing.

My dusty CRV was parked beside me, containing one restless dog and a variety of snack bags, all empty by now. There were no buildings in sight, no cars or people or movement at all. Only the constant humming of the insects as they buzzed around my head.

I turned to my left – another straight road that trailed off into the distance. I glanced over to the right, then behind me – two more barely discernible roads stretched out into the abyss. I was in a four-way intersection with no signs, no sense of direction, and no sign of life for several miles. No cell service either. *Damn*, I thought. *I'm lost.*

How did I get here? I couldn't help but feel like this little intersection was a cruel metaphor for life. I began to daydream, imagining each road might transport me back to a different time, a different role in my life, and a different me.

If I took the road from whence I came, it could lead me all the way back to Oregon, back to my cheating third husband, back to a life of loneliness and solitude. There is no greater loneliness than being married to someone who isn't actually present in your life.

If I took the road to my left, perhaps it could take me back to my career as a dental hygienist, a job I hated deep down in my soul. There is something so disengaging about cleaning teeth for a living. It's a disgusting, smelly way to get a paycheck. It pays well, which is great, but the best part is the huge gob of friends I enjoy to this day.

Or maybe the road to my right, *yes – maybe that's the path*, I imagined. Maybe it could take me back to my real treasure, my kids. Back to their smiling, innocent faces as toddlers, as they danced around the Christmas tree and their father and I were still married. Back when they still needed me for every little thing.

But, that was just it. I didn't feel needed anymore. My kids weren't toddlers anymore – they were both full-grown adults, and far too busy for me. My dental buddies were still working, but I wasn't. Dental hygiene had robbed me of the cartilage in my fingers, giving me severe, disabling arthritis. And, I wouldn't be returning to any more husbands either, because three marriages were quite enough for me.

All three of these paths, all three of these roles – the wife, the mother, and the dental hygienist – had seemingly been stripped from me within a year. I was lost and looking to find myself again.

The funny thing about this phrase, "not all who wander are lost" – is that, in my experience, wandering and being lost walk hand-in-hand with one another, and the expression can be flipped. In my experience, not all who are lost are wandering, and that is a real disservice to the beauty and clarity that the world has to offer.

When one becomes lost, wandering is the only option to guide oneself back to a path. After all, one could not come upon any dirt path at all without wandering.

I began wandering at an early age, both with my mind and with my feet. At eight years old, I was reading a book about archaeology and dreaming of one day seeing Egypt. I didn't follow a traditional path in high school either, going heavily into foreign languages, in hopes of one day using them.

At twenty-five years old, I divorced my first husband (the dental student who talked me into becoming a dental hygienist so I could work for him) and decided to give traveling a real shot. I took off for the Andes and Macchu Picchu, climbing up ancient Inca stone steps to reach the magnificent ruins.

Anyone who has been to Macchu Picchu will tell you there is something ethereal and deeply spiritual about the place. The ruins stretch out across the emerald green mountains, way up in the middle of the sky. Macchu Picchu gave me my first experience of feeling history. This trip inspired me to come back and complete a degree in archaeology, and I've been wandering ever since.

More travel followed including a backpack trip around Europe for three months, by myself, and trips to Britain, Italy, and Greece. I visited the burial places of Crusaders, mummies, and ancient kings. I happened upon the castle of my namesake in Bettendorf, Luxembourg, and wandered my way through European history.

My favorite excursion by far was finally seeing Egypt with my daughter in 2012. Just like my childhood dream envisioned, I rode a camel beneath the pyramids of Giza, with my head wrapped in some man's sweaty turban. It was perfect.

Traveling has always been my own personal antidote to pain. I went to Mexico after my first and second divorces, Canada after my third, and Italy after my dad died. Call it avoidance if you want, but I call it an accelerated form of healing in the purest sense of the word. I believe travel can heal your soul.

Wandering has always worked its wonders on me – made me feel renewed, rejoiceful, grateful, and purposeful. It's been my medicine.

So, as I stood in that intersection, I once again wondered how wandering had led me so astray this time. *What the hell am I supposed to do now?* It was then that I realized that one last path had not been considered yet – the path which stretched straight out in front of me. *Which role does this represent?* I pondered.

The answer smacked me in the face.

That last dirt road – the only path that could take me where I wanted to go, the only path that ever truly healed me or showed me the way – was the path of the traveler. The wife, the mother, and the hygienist roles – though valued in their time – were sitting in the bleachers now. It was time to welcome and enable my boldest, bravest, and perhaps most pivotal role yet:

The role of the Wandering Woman.

Welcome to Wandering Woman

This book is for you – the grieving empty nester mom, the begrudged housewife, the woman in need of a drastic change in her life. Really, this book is for anyone with a passion for traveling. If you feel lost with no sense of direction or purpose in life, that's a bonus – this book will be even more appealing to you. And lastly, if you're a man reading this book, congratulations for holding a book with the word woman in the title. You're contributing to gender equality, and that's pretty neat.

I decided to combine three of my dearest loves – travel, history, and archaeology – and put them into a book because I believe wandering has the power to change your life. I have been to many areas of the world and have enjoyed too many outstanding experiences to list. However, by the time both my children moved out in 2017, I realized I was a stranger in my own country. It was the perfect time to explore a new country (my own) and discover a new me at the same time. I have been traveling for five years now, and I've upgraded to a small RV. I also have a new traveling companion, another sweet Sheltie, named Rosie. ***Wandering Woman*** is the chronicle of my journey across the United States, discovering the joy of getting lost and finding myself along the way.

Why You Need to Take a Road Trip

*A**merica, the beautiful?*** I sure think so, but I didn't realize just how beautiful our country is until I embarked on traveling across the United States, full time, in a small RV.

The United States offers something for everyone. From spectacular beaches, austere mountains, to rolling plains, our country has it all. It's difficult to comprehend just how large and impressive our scenery is, until you experience it first-hand, with the ultimate road trip.

I also realized just how much of our history is missing from U.S. history I was taught as a kid. The history of our country didn't begin with the pilgrims landing on Plymouth Rock in the 1600s. Our history is far more ancient, with rock art and archaeological sites dating back over 12,000 years.

We owe a tremendous debt to early pioneers who tamed our land. The Mormons and other groups ventured into the great unknown with their families and their worldly possessions. Some of them pulled cumbersome handcarts across the country to settle in inhospitable, dangerous locations.

The goal of **Wandering Woman** is to bring history back to life and make it interesting again. I am presenting some famous sites, and many little-known ones. You will take the road-less-traveled with me, while we explore ghost towns, rock art sites, archaeological sites, and museums, to discover the colorful tapestry that is our country.

I present some history, including dates, but my goal is to present more of the real-life stories of history, including ghost stories, profiles in history, voices from the past, and moments in time, to give you, the reader, a deeper understanding of the context of history.

This is by no means an exhaustive list of places to visit. In fact, I encourage you to discover America for yourself, as I am doing, by making a trek across the land by car or RV. You can venture forth as the early explorers did, just a little more comfortably, with a lot less hardship.

I hope you enjoy this book and take a little time out to discover our beautiful country, and maybe even discover yourself in the process.

Safe Travels,

Julie Bettendorf

Welcome to Iowa

The Hawkeye State

*I**owa*** is at the crossroads of our country's history. It was first investigated by French explorers Father Jacques Marquette and Louis Joliet over 300 years ago. These explorers were followed by Zebulon Pike 132 years later. Early Native Americans were in Iowa hundreds of years before that, establishing amazing earthen mounds, including the world-famous Effigy Mounds. Today, you can enjoy the many friendly faces of people who are lucky enough to live in the great state of Iowa.

Five things to love about Iowa:

Pioneering and farming history from places like the Nelson Pioneer Farm

Underground railroad history from places like the Hitchcock House

Mysterious early Native American history from places like the Toolesboro Mounds

Scenic beauty of places like Bridges of Madison County

Riverfront history from places like Bonaparte

Dreams of Iowa

"What is it about Iowa? I'm the shortest guy in the state." **Jason Alexander**

"I am proud to have been born in Iowa. Through the eyes of a ten-year-old boy, it was a place of adventure and daily discoveries - the wonder of the growing crops, the excitements of the harvest, the journeys to the woods for nuts and hunting, the joys of snowy winters, the comfort of the family fireside, of good food and tender care." **Herbert Hoover**

"I think the only real knowledge I had before I went to Iowa was what I learned from Food Inc. But once I got there and developed these extensive relationships with the farmers, I realized that we're basically made of corn." **Zac Efron**

Famous People from Iowa

Black Hawk, Native American leader, (1767-1838)

Johnny Carson, entertainer, (1925-2005)

Buffalo Bill Cody, showman, (1846-1917)

Morgan Earp, lawmaker, (1851-1882)

Halston, fashion designer, (1932-1990)

Herbert Hoover, 31st President of the U.S. (1874-1964)

Glenn Miller, bandleader, (1904-1944)

John Wayne, actor, (1907-1979)

Elijah Wood, actor, (born 1981)

Early Iowa

Excavations at Turin

Sergeant Floyd's Grave 1895

Early Motor Town

Sergeant Floyd's Grave

*S*ergeant Floyd's Grave is America's first national monument. It commemorates Sergeant Charles Floyd from Kentucky, the only member of the Lewis and Clark Expedition to die on the journey. He most likely died of appendicitis and peritonitis. Expedition members buried him on a bluff overlooking the Missouri River.

The original memorial was a cedar post carved with the words "Sergt. C. Floyd died here 20th of August 1804." Eventually, erosion led to Floyd's bones being exposed, so he was reburied. He was buried a third time, and then buried a fourth time in 1901, and a sandstone obelisk was erected to honor him.

How to get to Sergeant Floyd's Grave:

Sergeant Floyd's Grave is located off Old Hwy. 75, just south of Sioux City, IA.

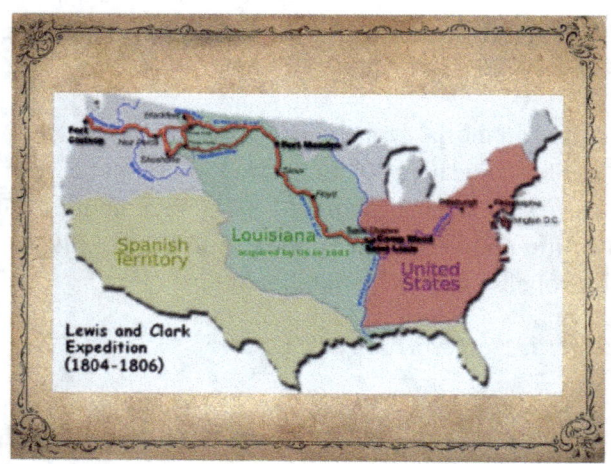

A word about Lewis & Clark's Corp of Discovery:

In 1803, President Thomas Jefferson funded the expedition with $2500. The group was to find the most direct water route to the Pacific. Meriwether Lewis, who was a family friend of Jefferson, was put in charge of the expedition. He enlisted his friend from the Indian campaigns, William Clark.

Meriwether Lewis and his men left Pittsburgh on 8/31/1803. They stopped in Clarksville, Indiana, to pick up William Clark and additional men. The group left St. Louis, Missouri, on May 15, 1804. When they left, Clark was 33, and Lewis was 29.

They spent their first winter among the Mandan tribe in North Dakota, establishing Fort Mandan. It was here that they added French explorer Charbonneau and his wife Sacajawea. They left Fort Mandan in April, 1805, heading up the Missouri river. They reached the Pacific Ocean in November, 1805. The journey would eventually take 28 months and the group would travel 8000 miles.
Jones

Facts about the Lewis & Clark Expedition:

Clark paid his interpreter Charbonneau a total of $500 and 33 and 1/3 cents for his services on the expedition.

There is a myth among the Nez Perce that the sister of Chief Red Grizzly Bear had a son with Clark. The boy had light hair and often proclaimed "Me Clark."

Venereal disease was common among the Indians they met. A few of the party suffered the effects from encounters with the women. Gonorrhea was a frequent problem, and what Lewis called Louis Venerae.

Sacajawea was promised to another Indian man, but because she had a child with Charbonneau, the Indian didn't want her. During the expedition, Charbonneau hit Sacajawea and was reprimanded by Clark.

Early in the expedition, several men were court-martialed and whipped for "having uttered repeated expressions of a highly criminal and mutinous nature," and desertion.

Clark suffered from foot problems, and Lewis suffered from depression.

During the expedition, the group endured hunger, disease, subzero temperatures, blizzards, fierce rapids, grizzly bear attacks, thick clouds of mosquitoes, and repeated robberies by Indians. They also were reduced to eating their dogs and colts to stay alive.

They wrote nearly one million published words in journals of their trip.

Only 1 out of 9 practicing doctors actually had a medical degree in Lewis & Clark's time. Most were trained on-the-job, including Lewis and Clark. Medications they took along included a variety of potent laxatives known as "Thunderclappers." They also brought along penile syringes to treat venereal disease by injecting a solution into the urethra.

Lancets were purchased for "therapeutic" bloodletting. Opium and a 10% opium solution known as Laudanum were used quite frequently on the trip. An ointment made of ground beetles was used to create blisters, believed to act as a "counterirritant" Lead acetate was used in "eyewashes" which were traded with Columbia Basin Indians.

The total cost of all medical supplies was $90.60. [Peck]

Voices from the past:

"...I am Dull & heavy been up the greater Part of last night with Serjt. Floyd, who is as bad as he can be to live... We came to make a warm bath for Sergt. Floyd hoping it would brace him a little, before we could get him into his bath, he expired, with a great deel of composure, haveing Said to me before his death that he was going away and wished me to write a letter... We buried him on the top of the bluff a Mile below a Small river to which we Gave his name, he was buried with the Honors of War, much lamented."
Journal of William Clark, 1804.

Profiles in history:

Charles Floyd was born in Kentucky between 1780 and 1785. His father and uncles fought under George Rogers Clark during the Revolutionary War. Floyd joined the Lewis and Clark Expedition at the Falls of Ohio, and was promoted to sergeant. After ninety-eight days of travel, Floyd became seriously ill. He died on August 20, 1804, and was buried by members of the expedition.

Turin

***T*urin** is an accidental archaeological site. The discovery
began in 1955, when a gravel pit operator uncovered a

skeleton. Soon archaeologists uncovered three more burials. Shell beads and stone artifacts were found with the skeletons.

The four skeletons found were of a young man about 20 years old, two children, ages 6 or 7, and 10 to 12, and an infant of about 4 to 5 months. They were buried in a flex position, with knees to the chest. One of the skeletons was adorned with red ochre.

Carbon dating indicates the site is from the Archaic period, and is 3000 to 6000 years old. The shell used in the beads comes from a freshwater snail, hundreds of miles from the Turin site.

How to get to Turin:

The Turin site is located on state hwy. 75 east of Onawa.

A Helpful Timeline:

The various periods of occupation in early North America can be confusing. Don't be surprised if you read slightly different dates from other sources, but these are some general guidelines to know about:

The Paleo-Indian Period, from 10,000 to 8500 BC, is characterized by hunting and gathering, and small family groups in temporary camps. Artifacts from this period include spears and darts.

The Archaic Period, from 8500 to 500 BC, is characterized by some cultivation, and small base settlements. Artifacts from this period include stone, shell, and copper items.

The Early Woodland Period, from 500 BC to 1 AD, is characterized by permanent villages, organization under a tribal or religious leader, and elite burials in mounds. Artifacts from this period include the addition of clay pottery.

The Middle Woodland Period, from 1 AD to 400 AD, is characterized by the introduction of maize, long-distance trade, and elite burials with precious objects. Burial mounds, platform mounds, and earthworks were built.

The Late Woodland Period, from 400 AD to 800 AD, is characterized by cultivated seed plants, large permanent villages, and use of the bow and arrow.

The Early Mississippi Period, from 800 AD to 1300 AD, is characterized by cultivation of corn, beans, and squash, with permanent villages and farming settlements. Temples and houses of leaders were built on mounds in major villages. Pottery and artistic forms were developed.

The Late Mississippi Period, from 1300 AD to 1700 AD, is characterized by towns enclosed in stockade walls, and increased power among chiefs and religious leaders. More elaborate artistic representations on pottery, shells, and wood became more common.

Fort Dodge
Museum

T he original ***Fort Dodge*** was established in 1850 as a row of buildings. No stockade was built. Instead, soldiers would ride out from the fort, patrolling the area. Members of the Dakota tribe came to the fort to trade.

Fort Dodge was abandoned by the Army in 1853, and bought by a man named William Williams, who used it as part of a planned community. He wrote detailed descriptions of the fort, including the presence of two Indian mounds on the parade grounds. One of these mounds was excavated in 1869, and human remains were found.

The Fort Dodge Museum contains a wonderful collection of historic buildings, including the Carlson-Richey Log Home, built in 1855.

Other historic buildings include The Ole Fjetland Cabinet Shop, Donahoe's General Store, the Colby Bros. Livery, the Opera House, a historic jail, and many others.

How to get to the Fort Dodge Museum:

The Fort Dodge Museum is located at 1 Museum Rd, in Fort Dodge, Iowa.

The Nelson Pioneer Farm & Museum

The Nelson Pioneer Farm & Museum is a wonderful 310 acre indoor and outdoor museum, containing a total of 15 buildings. The land was bequeathed in 1958 to commemorate John and Mary Nelson, parents of Daniel and Lillian Nelson, owners of the farm.

The grounds are beautiful and serene. You will see the Ivan Baker Windmill, built in 1880. It was originally located on a farm, near Indianapolis, Indiana.

One of my favorite buildings is the Benjamin Littler Cabin, built near Bussey, Iowa, between 1867 and 1869.

The 15 foot by 18 foot cabin housed Eenjamin and his wife Martha, and their four children. The logs are thought to have been cut and hewn by Benjamin.

The Daniel Nelson House was built in 1852 to 1853 using funds from the sale of Daniel's grist mill.

Nelson family members lived there until 1941. Log portions were built from trees on Nelson land, and bricks were made from clay on the banks of a creek nearby. The bricks were fired in a kiln on the farm.

During restoration work, contractors discovered a foundation stone containing engravings marking the quarry of John Colville (JC) Henry Walling, who may have helped lay the foundation (HAW) and "1852."

The Summer Kitchen was built in 1890 for the Nelson family. Meals were cooked outside to prevent fire and to help keep the main house cool.

My favorite area of the Nelson farm is the Mule Cemetery, the resting place of two historic mules, Jennie and Becky. The two mules were born in the 1840s and were sold to the US government in 1854. They hauled artillery during the Civil War. Daniel Nelson purchased the mules to work on his farm. According to legend, the mules are buried with satin pillows under their heads.

The Prine School House was opened in 1861 and cost $200 to build. The original building had two outhouses and a coal shed. A garage was added in the 1930s for the teacher's car. The schoolhouse remained in operation for 105 years, closing in 1966.

Other wonderful buildings include the Meeting House, Mott's General Store, Spring Creek Voting House, a doctor's office, and others.

Don't miss the delightful selection of curious goats on the property.

How to get to the Nelson Pioneer Farm and Museum:

The Nelson Pioneer Farm and Museum is located at 2211 Nelson Lane, two miles north of Oskaloosa, IA, off Hwy. 63.

The Hitchcock House

T he ***Hitchcock House*** is a stately stone structure built in 1856 by Congregationalist Minister George Hitchcock. It's a beautiful house, and also famous for being an important part of the underground railroad.

The Hitchcock House was a way station for escaped slaves headed to freedom. Abolitionist John Brown is said to have preached at the Hitchcock House.

The house is two stories, with walls 20 inches thick. The basement has two rooms, which were originally separated by a hinged cupboard. This cupboard was opened to gain access to a secret room where slaves could hide out.

The property also contains a historic Ferrry house, operated in the 1850s.

You will also see the lonely grave of 18 year old Leang Afa Hitch-cock, who was accidentally shot in 1856, while on a hunting trip.

How to get to the Hitchcock House:

The Hitchcock House is located at 63788 567th Lane, just outside of Lewis, Iowa.

A word about the Underground Railroad:

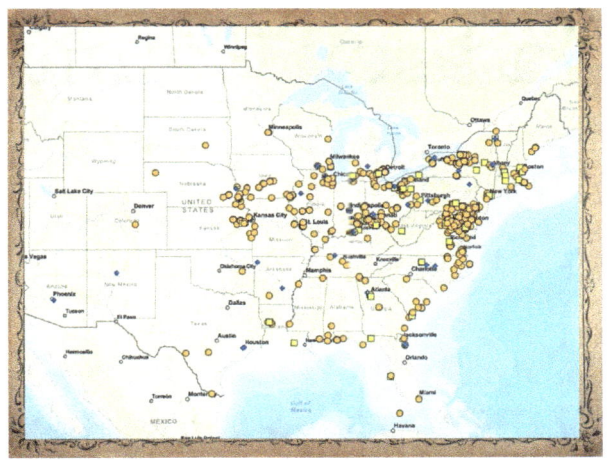

The Underground Railroad was a system of hideouts, known as stations, run by abolitionists and others dedicated to the end of slavery. Those aiding the slaves were known as conductors. The goal of the Underground Railroad was to aid in the safe transport of slaves from southern slave states into free northern states and Canada. Slaves began escaping north in the late 1700s, with the height of use occurring from 1830 to 1865. Patterned quilts were actually coded messages to give directions to the runaway slaves.

Bridges of
Madison County

I t is believed that at least 100 covered bridges were built across Madison County between 1850 and 1900. Flooding, fire, and demolition destroyed all but a few of the ***Bridges of Madison County***.

The Holliwell Covered Bridge was originally built in 1855 and was rebuilt in 1879. Measuring 155 feet, it is the longest covered bridge in the county.

The Cutler-Donahoe Covered Bridge was built in 1870 and is named after two early settlers to the area.

The Imes Covered Bridge was built in 1871. The bridge was later moved to its current location in 1977.

The Hogback Covered Bridge was built in 1884, and gets its name from the limestone ridge at the west end of the valley.

The Roseman Covered Bridge was built in 1883. Bridges were covered to protect them from weather and increase their life.

The Cedar Covered Bridge was bult in 1883 by H.P. Jones, who also built the Roseman Bridge. It was one of the last bridges built in Madison County.

How to get to the Bridges of Madison County:

To view and print a map of bridge locations, visit https://explore madisoncounty.com/covered_bridges/

Ghost story:

The Roseman Bridge is said to be the home of a ghost of an escaped convict. The convict was surrounded by a posse, which came in on both sides of the bridge. The man escaped, and his laughter has been heard near the bridge by locals.

Effigy Mounds

T he ***Effigy Mounds*** were created between 850 and 1400 years ago. The site contains 206 mounds, 31 of which are animal figures including bears, which were the most common, bison, lizards, and birds.

A typical effigy mound is 2 to 4 feet high, 40 feet wide, and 80 feet long.

The monument also contains cone-shaped mounds, which are the oldest and date back 2500 years. They were created by a culture known as the Woodland Culture.

The mounds were first surveyed in 1912. There are seven distinct mound groups containing 3 effigies, 42 conical mounds, 15 linear mounds, and a mound group containing buffalo effigies.

The Effigy Mounds are in a beautiful setting, right next to the river. Be sure to take time out to enjoy the views.

How to get to the Effigy Mounds:

The Effigy Mounds are located 3 miles north of Marquette on Hwy. 76.

A word about Indian Mounds:

Indian mounds were created in multiple shapes, including:

Conical mounds, which are round domes of earth; conical mounds contained burials, with the oldest mounds showing evidence of red ochre, which was used in the burials.

Linear mounds, which were 2 to 4 feet high, 6 to 8 feet across, and up to 100 feet long.

Compound mounds, which are a combination of conical mounds and linear mounds; these type of mounds are only found in the Effigy Mounds area.

Effigy mounds are found in Iowa, Southern Wisconsin, Northern Illinois, and Southeastern Minnesota.

Fort Atkinson

*F**ort Atkinson*** was established in 1840, and the fort's primary
function was to monitor the Ho-Chunk Nation, who were
forcibly moved from Wisconsin into Iowa. The fort was named for

Brigadier General Henry Atkinson, who promised to protect the Ho-Chunk Nation from enemies. He was also tasked to keep the Ho-Chunk, also known as the Winnebago, from moving back into Wisconsin.

Fort Atkinson was home to the dragoons, which were a mounted military force. It is estimated about 200 horses were also housed at the fort. Most of the buildings at the fort were built between 1842 and 1845. The fort was closed in 1849, when the soldiers went to fight in the Mexican-American War.

Today, as you walk around the fort, you can see the stockade walls. Originally these 11 foot 9 inch walls were tipped with iron.

The buildings include the two-story North Barracks, the eastern portion of which was the hospital. The first floor was the mess room, kitchen, and office of the Commandant. The dragoon soldiers lived on the second floor, sleeping 12 to a room, and 2 to a bed.

Another interesting building is the block house, built to defend against attack. The rifle slits are wider on the inside than the outside, making it possible for the soldiers to move right or left to fire, and making it harder for combatants to fire into the blockhouse.

You can also visit what remains of the St. James Lutheran Church, established at Fort Atkinson in 1871.

During archaeological investigations, recreational items including bone dominoes, clay pipes, and a jaw harp were found. Other artifacts included children's clay marbles, a writing slate, and a comb made of cow horn used to remove lice, which were a common problem at Fort Atkinson.

The soldiers did enjoy some luxuries. During a 1966 excavation of latrines and a bakehouse, English ceramics, French olive oil, German marbles, pipes, dominoes, musical instruments, and liquor bottles were found.

Fort Atkinson was abandoned in 1849, and cared for by an overseer until 1855, when it was sold of to area residents.

Don't miss the tranquil cemetery on the grounds of Fort Atkinson.

How to get to Fort Atkinson:

Fort Atkinson is located at 303 2nd St. NW in Fort Atkinson.

Motor Town

*M**otor*** is a lovely, scenic, abandoned town. Motor town was platted in 1875 and eventually had a few houses, a store, a school, an ice house, a tavern, and stables.

The massive mill building in Motor was built in 1868 and 1869, and cost $90,000 to construct.

A wooden bridge was built in 1868. A flood in 1883 laid waste to the town and the mill. The iron Pratt Bridge was built in 1898, after the flood.

Today you can see the mill building, a stable and livery, the stone inn, and the smokehouse.

How to get to Motor Town:

The ruins of Motor and Motor Mill are located 7 miles southeast of the town of Elkader, off Hwy. 13.

The Mines of Spain

The Mines of Spain recreational area was once the site of the Julien DuBuque estate, an area overseen by DuBuque in the 1780s. The area was deeded to DuBuque by the Spanish in 1796.

The Meskwaki tribe lived in the area and DuBuque established a friendly relationship with them. Through mutual cooperation, DuBuque and the Meskwaki mined lead, converting it into trade goods. The lead miners outlined a Miner's Compact, which was the first code of laws in Iowa, on the site in 1830.

When DuBuque died in 1810, the Meskwaki buried DuBuque in a log tomb, which didn't last. In 1897, settlers built an impressive stone tower which marks the DuBuque grave.

The Mines of Spain contain both Archaic and Woodland sites, dating back as far as 8,000 years. Mounds, village sites, and rock shelters are in the area.

How to get to the Mines of Spain:

The EB Lyons Interpretive Center for the Mines of Spain is located at 8991 Bellevue Heights Rd, in Dubuque.

Profiles in history:

Julien DuBuque was born on January 10, 1762 near Quebec, Canada. He was the first permanent settler in Iowa, establishing a trading post and lead mining in 1788, after he was given permission by the Meskwaki tribe. He received a land grant from the Spanish in 1796. He is thought to have married Potosa, the daughter of Fox Indian Chief Peosta. Dubuque died on March 24, 1810.

The Antoine
LeClaire House

The *Antoine LeClaire House* was built in 1853 on the bluffs above Davenport. LeClaire lived in the house until his death in 1861, and his family continued to reside in the house until 1881.

The house also functioned as a home for a Roman Catholic bishop, and a boardinghouse. The city of Davenport purchased the mansion in 1976.

Antoine LeClaire played an important role in Iowa history. He founded Davenport, which was the first large town in Iowa, began a ferry service across the Mississippi, became the first postmaster in Iowa, and helped found a bank.

William Clark, of the Lewis & Clark Expedition, mentored LeClaire. LeClaire became friends with all the major tribes in Iowa, and translated the autobiography of Black Hawk.

How to get to the Antoine LeClaire House:

The house is located at 630 E. 7th Street in Davenport.

Profiles in history:

Antoine LeClaire was born in 1797 in Michigan. He was Metis, the
son of a Canadian trader father and Potawatamie mother. As a
young child, Antoine learned many Native American languages,
allowing him to work as an interpreter and mediator later in
life. Antoine's father was captured during the war of 1812, and
William Clark cared for Antoine while his father was in captivity.
In 1820, Antoine married Marguerite LaPage, the daughter of a
Sauk leader, which gave him influence within the tribe. He died
in 1861.

Bettendorf

The town of ***Bettendorf*** holds a special place in my heart. It's my namesake, and the city has a rich history on its own. The town began under the name of Lillienthal in 1833, named for an early homesteading family. The town became Gilbert in 1858, named for a farmer who platted the town. Bettendorf became Bettendorf in 1903, when brothers William and Joseph Bettendorf moved their iron wagon factory to a site along the Mississippi, and the town was named after them.

The Bettendorf brothers expanded their production to include car manufacturing, and producing a luxury automobile called the Meteor. The Meteor was manufactured from 1907 to 1912, and could accommodate 7 passengers. It cost $3000, which was more money than a factory worker could make in a lifetime.

During World War II, the Bettendorf Company supplied equipment to the US Navy, which included mine sweepers and pro-
tective equipment. The US government purchased the truck plant
and began to manufacture tanks at the site. A division of the Bettendorf Company also produced the first bread slicing machine.

Each of the brothers built a mansion. I took a tour of the house of Joseph Bettendorf. The house was built in 1914-1915, has 28 rooms and is perched high on a hill, with a commanding view of the Mississippi riverfront.

The mansion contained a swimming pool, bowling alley, music room, and a ballroom. It also boasted 9 fireplaces, only one of which worked, because Joseph was afraid of fire.

There are wonderful details everywhere you look, including hand-painted wallpaper.

Back in the day, the needs of the Joseph Bettendorf family were
tended to by 15 servants.

The ***Bettendorf Mansion*** has many lovely features. My favorites are the elegant statues of the two dogs at the front of the house.

It was also way ahead of its time in 1915, with a central vacuum system. There is also an underground tunnel leading from the main house to the carriage house, where the carriages and horses were kept.

Older brother, William Bettendorf, also has a mansion in town. It's a spectacular Spanish style residence which is now a treatment facility, so I could not go inside. The house cost an amazing $125,000 back in 1910, and was built by European craftsmen, who were brought in to construct the mansion. One room in the mansion is paneled with wood from a single tree. Unfortunately, William never lived in the house. He died during an emergency surgery one week before he was to move in.

How to get to Bettendorf:

Bettendorf, Iowa is located in Scott County, in Eastern Iowa.

Profiles in history:

William Bettendorf was born in 1857 and became a machinist who invented a horse-lift plow and a metal wheel for farming equipment. By the age of 53, William held 94 patents. The success in his business life did not extend into his personal life. He suffered the deaths of his first wife and his two children. He died in 1910, before he could fully realize his business dreams.

Joseph Bettendorf was born in 1864 and became a machinist. He and his brother William founded the Bettendorf Company. He took over and managed the Bettendorf Company after William's death in 1910. Joseph died in 1933.

My story:

While I was in Bettendorf, Iowa, I went across the mighty Mississippi River to Moline, Illinois, and got caught in 80 mph winds. It was extremely hot outside, so my sweet dog, Rosie, and I waited out the winds, parking underneath an overpass. The windstorm turned out to be more widespread across 250 miles of the Midwest. Iowa and Illinois got a big piece of it. It was a rare storm, known as a derecho, and it caused millions of dollars in damage. Trees were upended, root ball and all. When I finally crept out from under the overpass, downed trees and power lines were everywhere. The Midwest is an adventure every day. Nature is powerful and we are like little mice next to its power.

Ghost story:

The ghost of a washer woman has been seen in Bettendorf. She was first seen in the 1800s, and has been reported to be accompanied by a wringer washer.

American Gothic House

T he ***American Gothic House***, also known as the Dibble House, was built in 1881 by Catherine and Charles Dibble. It provides the backdrop for the famous painting *American Gothic.*

American Gothic was painted in 1930 by Grant Wood, an Iowa artist. The models for the painting were Nan Wood, his sister, and Dr. Byron McKeeby, his dentist.

Interestingly, the two never posed together in front of the house, and they met for the first time 12 years after the painting was created.

How to get to the American Gothic House:

The American Gothic House is located at 300 American Gothic St, in Eldon, Iowa.

Profiles in history:

Grant Wood was born February 13, 1891 on a farm near Anamosa, Iowa. He always knew he wanted to be an artist. His first drawing was made on a piece of cardboard from a cracker box. He was sitting in the farm cellar, where he was shut in as punishment. He spent time at the Art Institute of Chicago, honing his skills as an artist. In 1918, he entered the military and painted camouflage on cannons. Wood traveled to France and studied at the Academie Julien in Paris. It was in Munich that he developed his unique Gothic style. Wood died of pancreatic cancer on February 12, 1942, one day before his 51st birthday.

Voices from the past:

"I want to reach everyday people, not just the art critics of the world." **Grant Wood**

Bonaparte

B*onaparte* is a gorgeous historic town, nestled next to the
Des Moines River. Just about every building in Bonaparte
is from the 1800s. It's also a famous crossing for the Mormon

pioneers. In fact, Brigham Young crossed the river here in March, 1846.

William Meek came to Bonaparte in 1836 and established a flour mill, which is now a restaurant. Many mills followed, all powered by magnificent water wheels along the river. Meek also operated a ferry, to move wagons, animals, and people across the river.

One of the most fascinating areas in Bonaparte is Bonaparte Pottery, which originally began as Parker-Hanbeck Pottery, which ran from 1866 to 1895.

Today you can see the original factory building from 1876 and purchase hand-crafted pottery pieces made from original 200 year-old molds.

Don't miss the historic Bonaparte Cemetery, established in 1838 by William Meek. The first burial was his son, Benjamin.

How to get to Bonaparte:

Bonaparte is located in Van Buren County, in Southeastern Iowa.

Voices from the past:

"There was a splendid Mill on the des Moines in this town (Bona-parte). The mill dam was built entirely across the river with lock to pass boats up and down. The River was beautiful and had a good ford with a rock bottom and was for a river of its size very convenient for travellers to ford at this time." **Hosea Stout, March 5, 1846**

Toolesboro Mounds

The first mention of the ***Toolesboro Mounds*** was in 1841, when John Newhall published a guide for emigrants to Iowa. Originally, the mounds averaged 20 to 30 feet high and had a circumference of 80 feet. There were originally 12 to 14 mounds at the site, and most were plundered by 1886.

Today, there are a total of seven mounds at the Toolesboro Mounds site, dating from 200 BC to 300 AD. The largest mound measures 100 feet wide and 8 feet high. The Hopewell created these mounds.

Excavations revealed copper, obsidian, marine shell, and mica artifacts, indicating the builders of the Toolesboro mounds had a vast trade network stretching from the Atlantic Coast and Great Lakes, and the Rocky Mountains to the Gulf of Mexico. Some of the mounds contained burials with rich grave goods.

How to get to the Toolesboro Mounds:

The Toolesboro Mounds are located 7 miles east of the town of Wapello off Hwy. 99.

Voices from the past:

"Upon the margin of this bluff...there are eight conical mounds, averaging from twenty to thirty feet in height, and about eighty feet in circumference at the base, with a small area or terrace upon their summits...A few feet in the rear, appear indistinct vestiges of the old fort, now almost obliterated by the work of time..."
from Sketches of Iowa or the Emigrants' Guide, by John B. Newhall, 1841.

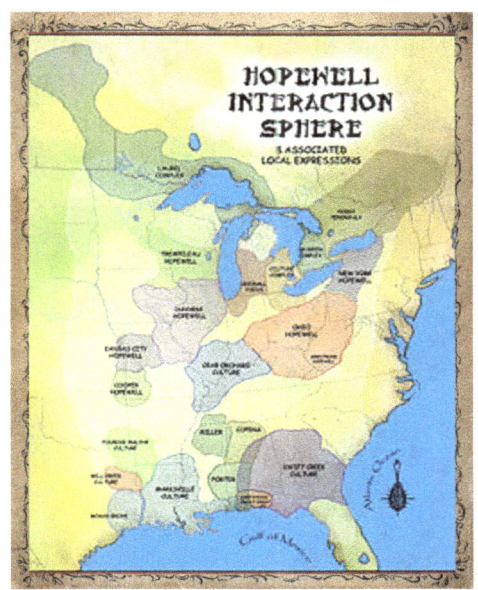

A word about the Hopewell tradition:

The ***Hopewell tradition*** gets its name from an archaeological site on a farm in the Ohio valley that belonged to Mordecai Hopewell. It is both a religious tradition, and a type of burial practice. Human remains could be placed lying down, or propped up, or some were cremated. Still others were left to decompose before they were buried.

Hopewell mound construction was stratified, with a layer of sand or clay on the floor, upon which the body and personal items were placed. Layers of earth, clay, sand, and gravel were placed and molded into a mound. Mounds often contain multiple burials of individuals placed in layers. Only the highest levels of society were buried within the mounds.

The Hopewell had an extensive trade network of copper tools, stone pipes, shell beads, and sheets of mica. The Hopewell tradition is not seen after 500 AD. The Hopewell could have merged with another culture.

Littleton Brothers Memorial

The ***Littleton Brothers Memorial*** delivers a poignant message. It memorializes six brothers, the children of James and Martha Littleton. These six young men all lost their lives during the Civil War. James and Martha Littleton came out west in 1840, settling near Toolesboro, where they had four daughters and six sons. Mother Martha died in 1853, and Father James died in 1860, neither living long enough to know what happened to their boys.

These are the Littleton boys:

Kendall, who died in 1862 at the Battle of Prairie Grove, in Arkansas. He was 20.

John, who was wounded and died in the same battle in 1862. He was 32.

Noah, who survived the battle but drowned in a ferryboat sinking. He was 17.

George, who was captured at Harpers Ferry. He was paroled from military prison because of illness and died in December 1862. He was 35.

William, who fought at Shiloh, Jackson, and Vicksburg. He died of disease in a hospital December 1863. He was 25.

Thomas, who survived the battles of Champion's Hill, Corinth, and Vicksburg, but was captured in Tennessee. He died at Andersonville Prison in Georgia in June 1864. He was 28.

How to get to Six Littleton Brothers Memorial:

The Littleton Brothers Memorial is located next to the Toolesboro Mounds, 7 miles east of Wapello, off Hwy. 99.

Fort Madison

***F**ort Madison* was the first fort established on the Upper
Mississippi River. It is the site of the Black Hawk battle
against the army. Fort Madison was established in 1808.

Several blockhouses were built to protect the fort, due to its vulnerable location. Attacks from Black Hawk became more frequent and severe during the war of 1812. The fort was abandoned in 1813.

Settlers arrived at the fort in the 1830s, and named their town Fort Madison, in honor of the fort.

Fort Madison is in a beautiful spot, right along the river, with a walking path nearby. Strolling around the barracks and block-house is a peaceful experience.

How to get to Fort Madison:

Fort Madison is located in Lee County, in Southeastern Iowa.

Favorite Places to Camp

L ake Ahquabi State Park is a large, beautiful place to camp. It's also centrally located, providing an excellent home base to tour Iowa. For more information or to make reservations, please visit https://iowastateparks.reserveamerica.com/camping/lake-a hquabi-state-park

Lake Keomah State Park is another of Iowa's spectacular camp-grounds, They offer full hookups and primitive sites, many of which are on a first come, first serve basis. For reservations, please visit https://iowastateparks.reserveamerica.com/camping/lake-k eomah-state-park

Random Thoughts
What History Means to Me

F irst, let me start by sharing with you my opinion of what history isn't. History is not a collection of random dates, names, and places for you to memorize. History is not a dry and uninteresting class you have to pass to graduate.

I believe history is a tangible thing. You can actually *feel* history in the places you go, and the sights you see. I remember walking up to the Acropolis in Athens. I looked down at the well-worn marble steps and wondered about how many ancient philosophers had climbed these very steps, thousands of years ago.

You don't have to go far away to experience the *feeling* of history. If you are lucky enough to live in an old house, you may experience history in your own surroundings. You might say to yourself, *"If only these walls could talk."*

During my travels across the United States, I *felt* history in many, many places. If you travel across the country like I did, you will *feel* the wonderful history of our beautiful country for yourself, and you will never be the same. You will discover what it means to be an American.

Why I travel, and why you should too:

I decided to travel across the country by car because I wanted to rediscover America. When I first set out to explore the history of our country, I wanted to find out why America is the greatest country on earth, and what it means to be an American.

The politics of these United States can be frightening and polarizing. I prefer to focus on what unites us, not what divides us. What unites us is we all live in a spectacularly beautiful country, with warm, wonderful people.

I began my journey five years ago, starting out in my Honda CRV. I soon realized I loved the lifestyle, so now I travel in a small RV. From my small RV, I look out on a country with a unique and colorful, multicultural tapestry, unlike any other country on earth.

I have a degree in Archaeology, and a passion for all things archaeological. I love history, with a side love of paleontology. It is these three passions that I set my trip agenda around. I set out to discover the archaeological sites, history, and paleontological world of our country.

As I travel and write my books, I get asked all the time, especially by women, "What is it like to travel by yourself? Aren't you scared?" The truth is, I believe everyone should do what I did. It's a wonderful way to discover our country, and to rediscover yourself. The truth is, I'm scared not to travel. Traveling allows you to get to know yourself, in ways not possible when sitting on the couch watching TV.

We tend to spend a lot of our lives tuning out the world and our place within it. When you travel, you are quite literally forced to deal with your own thoughts, emotions, and feelings. You can discover yourself while traveling. You can come to understand what makes you who you are, and how you can perhaps become a better person. Above all, traveling gives you mental clarity to figure out how to live with intent. It's a way to guide your life, not just wait for things to happen.

Travel Tips & Stuff
What You Need to Know

How to get started:

P lanning your trip should be one of the most exciting things about it. You want to be spontaneous, but it is also very wise to plan your route, so you can take full advantage of all the time and miles you will invest.

- First, decide your passions. If you love airplanes, trains, or old vehicles, plan your trip around that. If you love gardens or architecture, seek that out as the focus of your trip.

- Next, read and research areas of the country that will let you enjoy what you are interested in.

- Make a list by state and city or town, of what you want to see.

- Take your handy road atlas and locate the areas on the pages.

- Make a tentative route plan, so you have an idea of where you are going.

Travel tip: Avoid trying to plan your trip down to a schedule of days, hours, or minutes. On a road trip, it will be virtually impossible to know where you will be on any given day. If you adhere to a schedule, you are more likely to stress out, and less likely to actually enjoy yourself, which is the whole point.

What you need:

You need to bring along a sense of adventure and a curious mind. You need to ditch the idea of always being on a schedule, and live a little more spontaneously to thoroughly enjoy yourself. Things will happen as you travel, both good things and bad things, and you need to prepare your mind and your soul for day-to-day changes.

So much of our lives are planned out. Between growing up, going to school, finding a career, marriage, kids, or whatever, people have lost much of the ability to be spontaneous. But you must take spontaneity on the trip with you, because you may make detours along the way to see something really spectacular.

So, for the practical stuff you need:

A great vehicle-I am now five years into the trip and have swapped out my Honda CRV for a small RV, just under 20 feet. I go small because I see humongous RVs on the road, towing a car behind, and all I can think of is, they can't go just anywhere. They are too big. Bad gas mileage, cumbersome to drive, slow, and not agile like my small RV. So, I encourage you, if you want to go car or RV camping and be able to go on remote dirt roads, get an agile vehicle, and small RVs are great.

Travel tip: Don't be afraid to do some modifications to your vehicle. I have made many alterations to my RV, including changing the plumbing, which used to be a mere 4 inches off of the ground, so I would break it all the time. It's now encased in my outside storage compartment. I am also a minimalist, so I have jettisoned anything I won't use or don't love. Don't be afraid to get rid of unnecessary stuff.

An awesome camera that you know inside and out. I use a Nikon and it takes wonderful pictures. Don't skimp on a camera, and don't think a cellphone camera is all you need, because you want the best for your beautiful photos.

Window shades-the best ones are magnetic so you just place them against your windows and they cling to them, obscuring the view inside your car. I also have magnetic window screens, so I can leave my windows down with no bugs!

Battery operated fans and lights-these are important, so you don't have to rely on your house batteries for light and cooling options.

Portable air compressor-this little gem plugs into your cigarette lighter and will inflate your tires if you have a flat. Make sure the air compressor can reach to all of your tires, including your rear tires.

Portable battery charger and power bank-mine comes with battery cables and the power bank, yet once inside the case, it is small enough to put in your glove compartment. This little item, unfortunately, I have had to use, and it saved me.

Portable generator-I have two gas powered generators on the back of my RV, which are hooked together with a coupling unit. I have an interior generator, but after much expense and multiple repairs, it still doesn't work. Now I have generators which will run everything, including AC, and I can maintain them myself.

All season clothing-you never know what different states will bring for weather, so take hot weather and cold weather clothes, and a fair amount of shoes appropriate for hiking, or walking, sandals, and slippers, which are nice at night. Also take along a pair of cheap rubber flip-flops to wear in the public showers you might go into.

Your own pillows-I like my own pillows, so I don't wake up with neck cramps, especially after sleeping in the car.

Sleeping bag and cozy blankets -you want to stay warm and layering is everything.

Warm hat, warm socks, and fuzzy jammies to keep you warm for cold nights sleeping in the car.

A great road atlas, and great guidebooks-get one that's easy to read, with great pictures. For a road atlas, just get one that is easy to read.

A word about photography:

Along with a great camera, you need to have a great eye. This is easier than it sounds once you have worked with your camera and are comfortable taking pictures with it. I am not a professional photographer, but I like my pictures and other people do too.

These are my tips for taking great pictures:

- Experiment with taking both horizontal and vertical shots.

- Don't always put the subject of the photo in the middle of the photograph.

- This one is important: pay attention to the foreground, and if possible, have something, a plant or whatever, in the foreground to help give the photo dimension and depth.

- This one is important too: turn around often to see the view you just came from. I do this quite often and some of my best pictures have resulted from when I turned around and took the shot.

You can also take a mental photo. Place an image in your mind that you can call upon later. Use all of your senses to see, hear, smell, and maybe even to taste, what is around you. You have the means to fully experience your surroundings, and that is very important to a traveler. When you take a mental photo, be sure to jot down quick little details about what you saw, heard, smelled, or tasted, so you can jog your memory later.

And last, but not least...don't be posing in front of everything, everywhere, to show that you actually went somewhere. Most people want to see themselves in your photo and be mentally transported there, but they can't if you are there already.⌐

To camp or not to camp:

Car or RV camping is great. I prefer it to sleeping on the cold, hard ground in a tent. I can lock the doors, put my window shades up and be cozy for the night.

Some people camp in a Walmart parking lot and feel safe. I do not. I believe that if you are in a busy area, you are more likely to be confronted by a nut job who may bother you. Nothing against Walmart, and many Walmart stores don't allow overnight parking. I don't go for rest areas either because they have a track record of incidents happening to people in rest areas, especially women travelers.

I have come to love casino parking lots. I enjoy gambling, so for a little money, many casinos will provide overnight stays if you gamble a little inside the casino. I also do a lot of boondocking, because it's free, and I believe you are safer parked out in the middle of nowhere in the dark.

I also enjoy camping in state or national campgrounds, wildlife sanctuaries, and fairgrounds.

A word about safety:

When you are a woman traveling alone, it's critical to keep a low profile. Don't tell people you are traveling alone, where you are staying, or any other personal information.

I don't go to bars or get drunk. I'm not preaching but you are on your own, in a city or town you've never been to, and you don't know anyone, so it's not the time to lose control of what you are doing. When you are in control, you are better able to decide which people you want to get to know better.

Travel tip: If you feel vulnerable traveling alone, that's OK. Vulnerability is part of passion, and traveling is a passionate thing to do. You can put one of those family stickers on your vehicle to indicate to others that you are not traveling alone, which can help you feel more secure.

Maintain your connections:

When you are traveling alone, there is a definite sense of discon-nection. It feels almost like you are the only one in the world, traveling through space and time. That's why it's critical to keep your connections to loved ones active.

Be on Facebook while you are traveling. You may not have internet a lot of the time, or the internet will be poor. Consider paying to have your phone be a hotspot. It's a little bit of money per month, but it's worth it and has saved me from being without internet. I love the convenience of it, and you will too.

Plan your journey around visiting family members or friends you haven't seen for a long time, or people that are good friends. When you see people you know, it will ground you, so you can continue traveling.

Check in by phone with loved ones. They worry about you, and it's good for both of you to stay connected no matter where you are.

Consider traveling with a pet. I now travel with my 12 year-old sheltie Rosie, after losing my beloved sheltie, Sadie. Rosie is a wonderful companion. She is also an excellent watchdog, and barks her head off at other dogs and people.

Travel tip: One of the easiest and best ways I stay connected while traveling is to offer to take a photo for someone I don't know. Many couples, families, or singles would love to have more pictures of themselves traveling. It's an easy and quick way to have a connection with a fellow traveler, and it's good manners too.

Practical matters:

You need to have an address to send your mail to. Keep in touch with whomever is nice enough to do this for you.

You will also need to come back occasionally to register your car, vote, go to doctor visits, and take care of any other business. You can't leave it all behind, as tempting as that may be.

Bad things that happened:

I have had a few problems, mostly associated with my RV. I bought an older model, vintage 1999, and I have had to do a few repairs.

My worst experience came when I took my rig in to a shop in Spokane, Washington (who shall remain nameless.) All I needed was an oil change. I got the oil change and was about an hour south of town on a Friday at 4:30, when my engine blew.

I was in the middle of the eastern Washington prairie, many miles from the nearest town. All I could do was watch my oil drain out onto the Interstate. I can't help but think it was associated with my oil change, but I couldn't prove it. The moral of this story is: DON'T LET JUST ANYONE WORK ON YOUR VEHICLE.

Good things that happened:

I have met many great people on my travels, from all walks of life. I have also learned not to judge people. I have met numerous homeless people who are often just wanting a kind word, and not to be treated like dirt.

People have mistaken me for a homeless person, and I too, have been treated like dirt. When I can, I try to help people and be kind to them. Most of the time, they smile and reciprocate. You will always meet people who are unkind, but they are just as likely to be driving a huge expensive rig, or to be homeless.

We are all Americans, and we are all part of the human race. When you meet people across the country, you realize just how important it is to get to know your fellow citizens, and learn more about how they view the world and our country.

I have to give a special shout-out to the many dedicated people, often volunteers, who staff our state and national parks and monuments. They work tirelessly to ensure the health of our natural resources, and help travelers enjoy their visit. The same is true of the many people who staff the museums in small towns and large cities. They enjoy history, like I do, and it shows in their smiles.

Along with wonderful people, I have seen an America that is spectacularly beautiful, with open prairies, majestic mountains, and crystal clear rivers. I have seen a small fraction of the history of our country. I have seen the memorials to the brave people who shaped our country. I have fallen in love with America in a way that was not possible sitting in my living room. People ask me, "would I do it again?" The answer comes easily, "Yes, in a heartbeat."

Bibliography
For Further Reading

America Revealed, Life Books, 2012.

Collins, David, et. al, *Bettendorf, Iowa's Exciting City*, Arcadia Publishing, 2000.

Finch, etc. al.., Jackie. *Eyewitness Travel USA*. DK Publishing,2017.

Jones, Landon Y. *The Essential Lewis and Clark*, Harper Collins Publishers, 2000.

Lewis and Clark National and State Historical Parks, National Park Service.

McCarty, Michael, McLaughlin, Mark, *Ghosts of the Quad Cities*, History Press, 2019.

Nelson Pioneer Farm & Museum Visitors Brochure.

Nelson Pioneer Farm, Visitors Map.

Peck, David J. *Or Perish in the Attempt: The Hardship and Medicine of the Lewis and Clark Expedition,* The History Press, 2002.

Whittaker, Alex, De La Garza, *The Archaeological Guide to Iowa*, University of Iowa Press, 2015.

Index

Referenced by Sections

A

B

Battle of Prairie Grove-see Littleton Brothers Memorial

Becky and Jennie, pioneer mules-see Nelson Pioneer Farm

Benjamin Littler Cabin-see Nelson Pioneer Farm

Bettendorf Company-see Bettendorf

Bettendorf, Joseph-see Bettendorf

Bettendorf, William-see Bettendorf

Black Hawk-see Famous People from Iowa, Antoine LeClaire House, Fort Madison

Bonaparte Pottery-see Bonaparte

Brown, John-see Hitchcock House

C

Carlson-Richey log house-see Fort Dodge

Carson, Johnny-see Famous People from Iowa

Cedar Covered Bridge-see Bridges of Madison County

Chief Peosta-see Mines of Spain

Civil War-see Nelson Pioneer Farm, Littleton Brothers Memorial

Clark, George Rogers-see Sergeant Floyd's Grave

Clark, William-see Antoine LeClaire House

I

Imes Covered Bridge-see Bridges of Madison County

Ivan Baker Windmill-see Nelson Pioneer Farm

L

LaPage, Marguerite-see Antoine LeClaire House

Late Mississippi period-see Turin

Late Woodland period-see Turin

LeClaire, Antoine-see Antoine LeClaire House

Lewis and Clark Expedition-see Sergeant Floyd's Grave

Lillienthal-see Bettendorf

Littleton, George-see Littleton Brothers Memorial

Littleton, James and Martha-see Littleton Brothers Memorial

Littleton, John-see Littleton Brothers Memorial

Littleton, Kendall-see Littleton Brothers Memorial

Littleton, Noah-see Littleton Brothers Memorial

Littleton, Thomas-see Littleton Brothers Memorial

Littleton, William-see Littleton Brothers Memorial

M

N

O

Ole Fjetland Cabinet Shop-see Fort Dodge

P

Paleo-Indian period-see Turin

Parker-Hanbeck Pottery-see Bonaparte

Potosa-see Mines of Spain

Pratt Bridge-see Motor Town

Prine School House-see Nelson Pioneer Farm

Profiles in history-see Sergeant Floyd's Grave, Mines of Spain, Antoine LeClaire House, Bettendorf, American Gothic House

R

Roseman Covered Bridge-see Bridges of Madison County

S

Sergeant Floyd's Grave-see Early Iowa

Spring Creek Voting House-see Nelson Pioneer Farm

St. James Lutheran Church-see Fort Atkinson

Stout, Hosea-see Bonaparte

Summer Kitchen-see Nelson Pioneer Farm

About the Author

Julie Bettendorf is a world traveler with a degree in archaeology and a background in history. She has traveled extensively throughout Egypt, Central America, South America, Europe, and the United Kingdom, visiting archaeological and historical sites all along the way.

Currently, Julie is traveling around the US visiting ghost towns, ancient rock art sites, and archaeological wonders as part of research for her ongoing historical travel series entitled *Wandering Woman*. Wandering Woman is a set of state-by-state guides, full of photographs, historical anecdotes, and unique tips to help other women travel and explore solo across the US by car or RV. Julie enjoys writing freelance blogs, traveling frequently with her two adult children, and hiking outdoors with her faithful dog companion Rosie.

Also by Julie Bettendorf

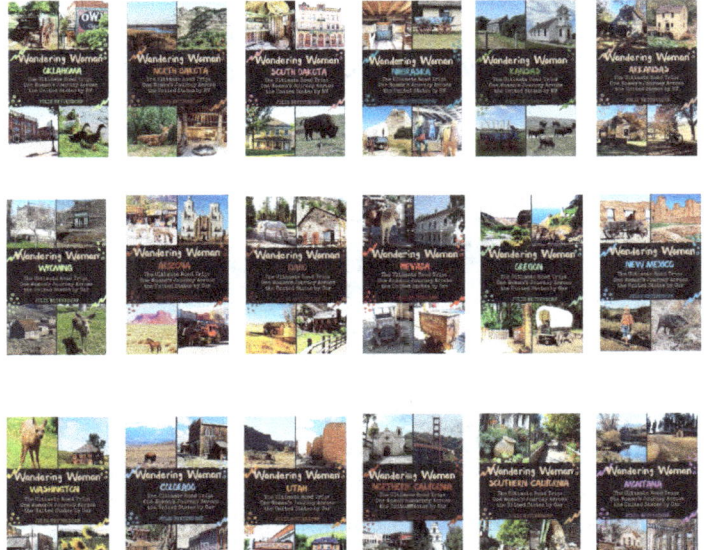

Wandering Woman: Iowa is the most recent book in the ***Wandering Woman Travel Series,*** available in both ebook and paperback.

Julie has published two children's books in an ongoing, beautifully illustrated travel series entitled ***Anthony Ant Goes to France*** and ***Anthony Ant Goes to Egypt***.

She has also published a work of historical fiction entitled ***Luxor: Book of Past Lives*** which has recently been released as an audiobook, read by renowned narrator Barry Shannon.